LET'S TALK SPORTS!

TALK LIKE A FOOTBALL PLAYER

BY RYAN NAGELHOUT

Gareth Stevens
PUBLISHING

Please visit our website, www.garethstevens.com. For a free color catalog of all our high-quality books, call toll free 1-800-542-2595 or fax 1-877-542-2596.

Cataloging-in-Publication Data
Names: Nagelhout, Ryan.
Title: Talk like a football player / Ryan Nagelhout.
Description: New York : Gareth Stevens Publishing, 2017. | Series: Let's talk sports! | Includes index.
Identifiers: ISBN 9781482457001 (pbk.) | ISBN 9781482457025 (library bound) | ISBN 9781482457018 (6 pack)
Subjects: LCSH: Football–Juvenile literature. | Football players–Juvenile literature. | Football–Terminology–Juvenile literature.
Classification: LCC GV950.7 N34 2017 | DDC 796.332'64–dc23

First Edition

Published in 2017 by
Gareth Stevens Publishing
111 East 14th Street, Suite 349
New York, NY 10003

Copyright © 2017 Gareth Stevens Publishing

Designer: Samantha DeMartin
Editor: Ryan Nagelhout

Photo credits: Title art chudo-yudo/Shutterstock.com; series background Supphachai Salaeman/Shutterstock.com; cover, p. 1 inset EKS/Shutterstock.com; cover, p. 1 football player Erik Isakson/Getty Images; football caption Mtsaride/Shutterstock.com; p. 5 David Lee/Shutterstock.com; p. 6 Raymond Boyd/Michael Ochs Archives/Shutterstock.com; p. 7 Phonlamai Photo/Shutterstock.com; pp. 8, 19 antpkr/Shutterstock.com; p. 9 Doug Benc/Getty Images Sport/Getty Images; p. 10 adoc-photos/Corbis Historical/Getty Images; p. 11 Joe Robbins/Getty Images Sport/Getty Images; p. 13 Lowe Llaguno/Shutterstock.com; p. 14 Rich Barnes/Getty Images Sport/Getty Images; p. 15 Jonathan Daniel/Getty Images Sport/Getty Images; p. 16 RonTech3000/Shutterstock.com; p. 17 Michael Zagaris/Getty Images Sport/Getty Images; p. 18 Maddie Meyer/Getty Images Sport/Getty Images; p. 21 Aina Jameela/Shutterstock.com; p. 22 Bob Levey/Getty Images Sport/Getty Images; p. 23 Tom Szczerbowski/Getty Images Sport/Gettty Images; p. 25 John Grieshop/Getty Images Sport/Getty Images; p. 26 Mike Flippo/Shutterstock.com; p. 27 Grant Halverson/Getty Images Sport/Getty Images; p. 29 Jim Rogash/Getty Images Sport/Getty Images.

Printed in the United States of America

CPSIA compliance information: Batch #CW17GS : For further information contact Gareth Stevens, New York, New York at 1-800-542-2595.

CONTENTS

Words in the glossary appear in **bold** type the first time they are used in the text.

TAKE TO THE TURF

Football is the most popular sport in the United States for a reason. It's a great sport to watch and really fun to play! But it isn't always easy to talk about. How much do you know about football?

Do you know why a football field is called the turf? And what's a football, anyway? If you want to talk like a football player, you'd better read on to find out!

TODAY'S FOOTBALL IS SHAPED LIKE A PROLATE SPHEROID—AN OVAL SHAPE THAT HAS TWO POINTED ENDS.

LEARN THE LINGO

"Turf" is a field that is artificial, or not made of real grass. Early forms were called AstroTurf or Tartan Turf, and today's artificial turf is often called FieldTurf.

TAKE THE FIELD

Football is a game measured in yards. There are 100 yards (300 feet) marked on an American football field, but it's actually 120 yards long! That's because the field has a 10-yard end zone at each end. This is where teams need to get the ball to score.

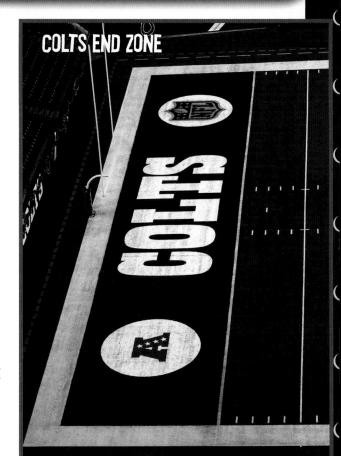

COLTS END ZONE

AN AMERICAN FOOTBALL FIELD IS 53 YARDS WIDE. OTHER TYPES OF FOOTBALL, LIKE THAT PLAYED IN CANADA, ARE PLAYED ON A LONGER AND WIDER FIELD.

ON THE LINE

Short lines painted on the field mark off each yard. Long lines stretching across the width of the field mark off every 5 yards. Big numbers mark every 10 yards on the field.

LEARN THE LINGO

The center line on a field is called the 50-yard line. Numbers start at each end zone and count up to 50 by 10s.

ON THE SIDE

Lines on the ground mark off the field of play. Anything inside the 100-by-53-yard rectangle—or in the end zones—is in play. Anything outside that is called "out of bounds." The long lines that mark out of bounds down the length of the field are called sidelines.

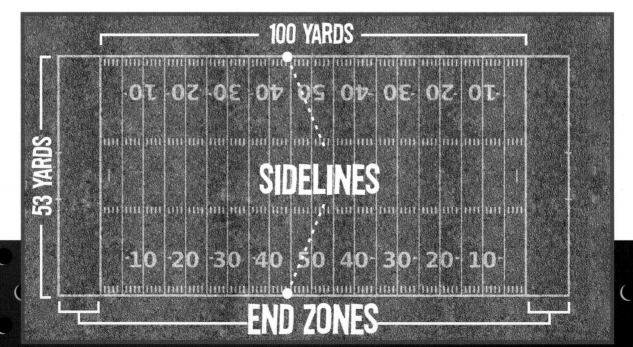

100 YARDS

53 YARDS

SIDELINES

END ZONES

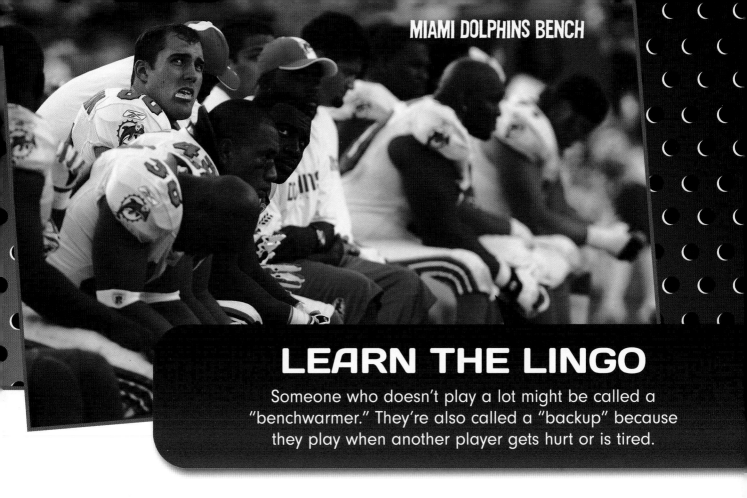

MIAMI DOLPHINS BENCH

LEARN THE LINGO

Someone who doesn't play a lot might be called a "benchwarmer." They're also called a "backup" because they play when another player gets hurt or is tired.

HIT THE BENCH

Each team gets one sideline for players and **coaches** to stand on when they're not on the field. There are **benches** where players can sit, and people working with the team can help players there if they get hurt.

WHAT'S A FOOTBALL, ANYWAY?

The name "football" came from "rugby football," the sport American football grew out of. Rugby also has end zones where teams score, but the rules and game are very different. The first rules for American football were written in 1876. The game has changed a lot since then!

RUN OR THROW?

One big change is the forward pass. A player called a quarterback can throw the ball to a player called a receiver to advance the ball. Before that, you could only run with the ball up the field.

QUARTERBACK AARON RODGERS

LEARN THE LINGO

In other countries around the world, soccer is called "football," and football is called "American football." The word "soccer" comes from the term **"association** football," or "assoc."

11

10 TO GO

Football is a game of yards and **downs**. The team trying to gain yards is the offense, and the team trying to stop them is the defense. Each offense has four tries, or downs, to gain 10 yards. They do this by running different plays, which have a player run with or throw the ball.

 PEOPLE HOLD MARKERS ON THE SIDELINE THAT TELL PLAYERS WHAT DOWN IT IS. THEY ALSO MARK THE POINT ON THE FIELD A TEAM NEEDS TO REACH FOR A NEW FIRST DOWN.

COUNT TO FOUR

The attempts to gain 10 yards are called first down, second down, third down, and fourth down. If the team trying to move the ball gains 10 yards, they get a new set of downs.

LEARN THE LINGO

When talking about downs and yards, people always say the down first. Every **drive** starts at "first and 10." If a team gains 3 yards on first down, they're at "second and 7."

13

The offense tries to move the ball down the field toward the defense's end zone. If they get the ball across the goal line and into the end zone, they've scored a touchdown!

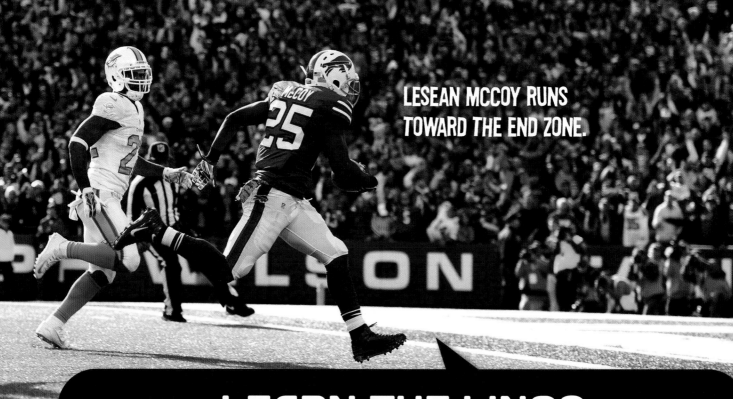

LESEAN MCCOY RUNS TOWARD THE END ZONE.

LEARN THE LINGO

Giving the ball to the defensive team is called a turnover. When a team doesn't get a new first down on fourth down, it's called a turnover on downs.

PUNTING IS WINNING?

If a team reaches fourth down, they must choose: go for a new first down or punt. If they try for the first down and fail, the defense gets the ball and might be in position to score. Or they could punt—kick the ball down the field to the defense, pushing them farther away from scoring.

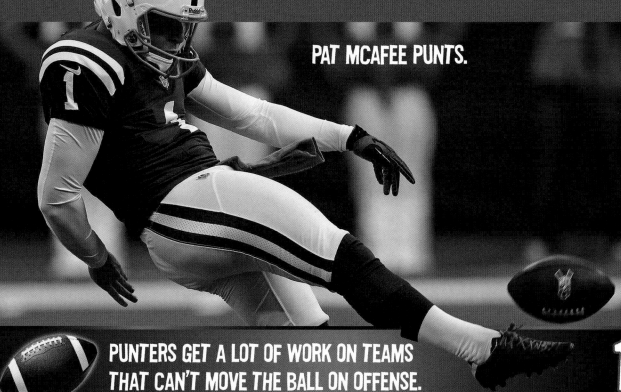

PAT MCAFEE PUNTS.

PUNTERS GET A LOT OF WORK ON TEAMS THAT CAN'T MOVE THE BALL ON OFFENSE.

15

KEEPING TIME

A standard football game is 60 minutes long.

It's broken up into four quarters, with each quarter lasting

15 minutes. The first
and second quarters
are called the first half.
The third and fourth
quarters make up the
second half.

THE SCOREBOARD AT A FOOTBALL GAME IS VERY IMPORTANT. IT KEEPS TRACK OF POINTS, DOWNS, YARDS, AND MORE FOR EACH TEAM.

LEARN THE LINGO

If the game is tied at the end of the fourth quarter, they keep playing. This is called overtime. Different leagues have different rules for overtime, but teams keep playing until someone wins!

CUT IT IN HALF

After the second quarter is finished, the teams stop playing for a bit. This is called halftime. Both teams leave the field and head for the **locker room**, where they take a break and talk about the game before the second half starts.

17

PLAYS AND PLAYERS

Each team has 11 players on the field. These players match up against one another on offense and defense. The offensive line tries to keep the defensive line away from the player carrying the ball.

WILL ALLEN TACKLES TOM BRADY.

LEARN THE LINGO

The defense tries to **tackle** the person with the ball. A play ends when the ball carrier is tackled, runs out of bounds, or scores a touchdown!

EACH PLAYER ON THE FIELD HAS A SPECIAL NAME BECAUSE THEY DO DIFFERENT THINGS. DIFFERENT TEAMS USE DIFFERENT NUMBERS OF PLAYERS AT CERTAIN POSITIONS.

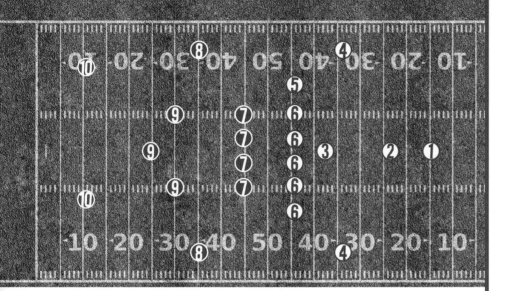

OFFENSE
1. RUNNING BACK
2. FULLBACK
3. QUARTERBACK
4. WIDE RECEIVER
5. TIGHT END
6. OFFENSIVE LINE

DEFENSE
7. DEFENSIVE LINE
8. CORNERBACK
9. LINEBACKER
10. SAFETY

SNAP IT

Each play on offense starts with the snap. That's when the center snaps the ball backward between their legs to the quarterback. The quarterback then throws the ball to a wide receiver, hands it to a running back to run with it, or keeps it and runs with it.

19

WAYS TO SCORE

Football scores can look very different based on what kind of scoring plays each team completes. A touchdown, for example, is worth 6 points. Teams can then kick a point after touchdown (PAT), or extra point, for a total of 7 points.

LEARN THE LINGO

Goalposts in each end zone are used for kicking points. If the ball goes between the **uprights** for a PAT, it's worth one point. If it goes through the uprights on any other down, it's worth three. This is called a field goal.

FIELD GOAL

POINT AFTER TOUCHDOWN

TWO-POINT CONVERSION

TOUCHDOWN

SAFETY

THESE ARE THE DIFFERENT WAYS YOU CAN SCORE POINTS.

GO FOR TWO!

They also have the **option** to try a two-point **conversion**.

The offense gets the ball at the 2-yard line and has one

chance to run a play that puts the ball in the end zone.

That makes a touchdown worth a total of 8 points!

If a defender catches a quarterback's throw, it's called an interception. This is another kind of turnover a defense can score on. If the defender is tackled before the end zone, that team's offense gets to start a drive there.

JJ WATT RECOVERS A FUMBLE.

Defenses can score points, too! This usually happens on turnovers. If a ball carrier drops the ball, this is called a fumble. Defenders can pick up the ball and run it into the end zone for a touchdown!

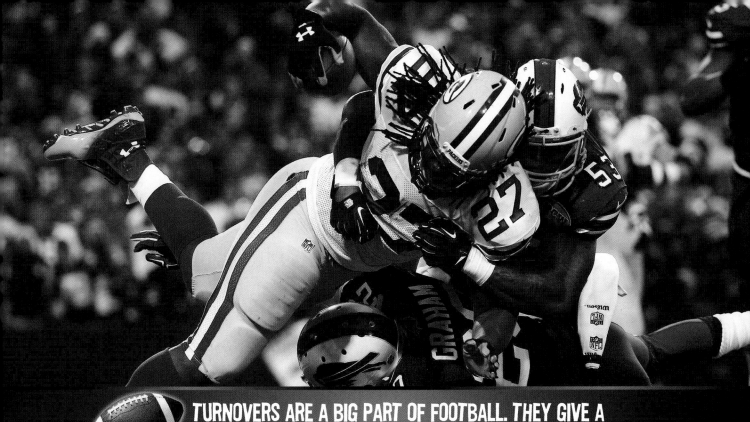

TURNOVERS ARE A BIG PART OF FOOTBALL. THEY GIVE A TEAM'S OFFENSE MORE CHANCES TO SCORE POINTS!

SAFETY!

If a defensive player tackles a ball carrier in their own end zone, it's called a safety! The defense's team gets two points, and the offense gets the ball back. It's also a safety if the ball goes through the back of the end zone on a fumble.

23

SPECIAL TEAMS

Each team has players that work on kicking and punting plays. They're on special teams! On kickoffs, the kicking team players quickly run down the field to chase the ball carrier while the other team's special teams players try to block.

KICKS AND PUNTS

Special teams players protect the kicker on field goals and PATs. They also try to tackle (or defend) the ball carrier on a punt. These players are good at blocking, or keeping defending players from reaching the ball carrier.

LEARN THE LINGO

If the kickoff goes into the end zone, and the returner doesn't run it out, it's called a touchback.

BRANDON TATE RETURNS A KICKOFF.

 KICKOFFS START EACH GAME'S HALF. THIS IS ALSO HOW A SCORING TEAM GIVES THE BALL TO THE OTHER TEAM AFTER A SCORING PLAY.

PENALTIES

Officials are the people in charge of making sure teams follow the rules of football. Officials are also called referees. There are different kinds of referees who watch plays from different parts of the field. Referees blow a whistle when a play has ended.

OFFICIALS DO DIFFERENT THINGS WITH THEIR HANDS WHEN THEY START THE GAME CLOCK OR CALL PENALTIES.

YELLOW FLAG

When a player does something against the rules, officials throw a yellow flag in the air. They then explain what rule the player broke. This is a penalty. There are lots of different penalties players need to avoid.

LEARN THE LINGO

Penalties add or take away yards needed for a first down. Some give teams a new set of downs. This is called an "automatic" first down!

TRICKS OF THE TRADE

Football is a game with a lot of rules. There's plenty more to learn about how to play. Did you know teams don't always have to give the ball to the other team? An offense might try a fake punt to try getting enough yards for a first down!

LEARN THE LINGO

Anyone on offense can throw the ball forward if they do it before the yard mark where the ball was snapped. This is called the line of scrimmage.

TRICK PLAYS

Coaches sometimes will try trick plays to catch the defense off guard. A running back could toss the ball back to a quarterback to throw a pass. Sometimes a running back will throw the ball, too!

RILEY COOPER BATS AN ONSIDE KICK.

A SHORT KICKOFF THE KICKING TEAM TRIES TO RECOVER IS CALLED AN ONSIDE KICK.

GLOSSARY

association: a group with similar interests

bench: an area where players not on the field can sit and watch the game with teammates

coach: a person who instructs or trains a team

conversion: the making of a score on a try for points after a touchdown in football

down: an attempt to advance the ball in football

drive: an offense's attempt to move the ball down the field to score

locker room: a room for changing clothes and resting used by sports players

option: the right to choose one thing or another

tackle: to grab a player and throw them to the ground

upright: one of the two poles pointed to the sky on football goalposts